THE LITERAL INTERPRETATION
OF
THE SERMON ON THE MOUNT

BY

MARCUS DODS, D.D.
JAMES DENNEY, D.D.
JAMES MOFFATT, D.D.

LONDON
HODDER & STOUGHTON
1904

First published London 1904 by Hodder & Stoughton.
This edition published in Ireland 2017 by <u>CrossReach Publications</u>.

Available in paper and electronic editions. A few select titles are also being published as audiobooks. Please go online for more great works available through CrossReach Publications. If you enjoyed this edition and think others might too, then consider helping us out by leaving a review online, mentioning us by name.

CONTENTS

NOTE

THESE Chapters were originally published in the *British Weekly* in 1904, as the result of the correspondence in its columns, and are now reprinted by request.

THE LITERAL INTERPRETATION OF THE SERMON ON THE MOUNT

I

BY THE REV. PROFESSOR MARCUS DODS, D.D.

THE abundant correspondence which has been appearing in these columns fairly represents the variety of opinion at present held regarding some of our Lord's precepts. Some think that as St. Paul's injunctions regarding the dress and conduct of women, or St. James's regarding the anointing of the sick, have become obsolete through the alteration of circumstances, so if our Lord had lived in our social conditions He would have used different language for the guidance of His followers. Others hold that His language was intended to be and is binding for all time and all conditions, and that the Church can never fulfil the function of salt to the world until these precepts are literally obeyed. Many a humble Christian, anxious to discover why the world is no better and happier, and why the religion of Christ does so little to mend it, reads the Sermon on the Mount, and says: Here is the secret: men have not obeyed Christ. Here are precepts which the Church ignores. Christianity has not moved the world for the simple reason that Christianity as Christ meant it does not exist in the world, but only a spurious, degenerate, pithless imitation of it.

Needless difficulties have been introduced by mere misunderstanding or over-scrupulosity. Our Lord's prohibition of oaths has been interpreted by the Society of Friends in such a sense that they refuse to take an oath even in a court of justice. When George Fox was commanded by the Judges at Lancaster to take the oath, he replied: 'Ye have given me a book here to kiss and to swear on, and this book which ye have given me to kiss says, "Kiss the Son," and the Son says in this book, "Swear not at all." Now I say as the book says, and yet ye imprison me; how chance ye do not imprison the book for saying so? How comes it that the book is at liberty amongst you, which bids me not swear, and yet ye imprison me for doing as the book bids me? Why don't ye imprison the book?' But what our Lord is protesting against is not the taking of an oath in a court of justice, or the swearing of fealty to an Emperor, but the Oriental habit of interlarding the whole conversation with what we euphemistically call 'strong language.' The accepted distinction between the typical Oriental and the Anglo-Saxon is the false and lying habit of the one, the frankness and truth of the other. But where lying is the habit a statement is accepted only when accompanied by the strongest asseverations. Hence the constant use of oaths in conversation. Where we should content ourselves with a simple 'Is it possible?' or a bare 'Indeed?' the Arab says 'Wallah,' that is, 'By God,' or 'Do you say that on oath?' Among ourselves swearing is commonly the inarticulate emphasis of ignorance, and is used by persons who do not know their mother-tongue sufficiently well to be articulately and intelligently emphatic. As Carlyle says of his father: 'In anger he had no need of oaths, his words were like sharp arrows that smote into the very heart.'

That this simplicity of language, the natural accompaniment of truthfulness, should suffice in a court of justice is, no doubt, desirable, but while many of those who appear in courts are notoriously untruthful, it is legitimate to use means for reminding them of the sacredness of truth. St. Paul on urgent occasion did not scruple to confirm his statements with an oath, 'I call God to witness upon my soul.' And as the writer to the Hebrews assures us, we have God's own example in using an oath for confirmation and for the end of all strife.

Similarly, when we read the injunction, 'Give to him that asketh thee, and from him that would borrow of thee turn not thou away,' it at once occurs to us that there are two quite different classes of persons who seek loans. There are persons of slender means or no means at all, women too old, or too delicate, or too inexperienced to cope with the world except at a great disadvantage, friends in a temporary difficulty, and those countless cases of genuine need which are constantly arising; and there are, on the other hand, the wholly different classes of persons who want money to push a public undertaking or for their own commercial benefit. To treat those two distinct classes alike would be unjust. To require interest in the one case is a cruelty; in the other, a perfectly legitimate commercial transaction.

The general precept, 'Resist not evil,' has created more difficulty than any of the others. Certainly it was meant to warn us against vindictiveness. It is directly and explicitly opposed to the *lex talionis*, 'An eye for an eye, a tooth for a tooth.' In some respects therefore it is one of the most characteristic injunctions, signalising, as it does, the transition from a bare, rigid, and inhuman legalism to an era of forgiveness and love. And it is amazing how much ground this reasonable view of human relations has already gained. The blood-feud, the vendetta, the duel, once considered legitimate, honourable, and compulsory, are now in Christian countries abolished or discountenanced. And this gives good promise that the improvement in individual relations will be followed by amelioration of those that are national, and that war, which rarely satisfies either party, will be superseded by friendliness and reason.

At the same time it is evident that the injunction cannot be accepted as an absolute law, valid in all circumstances. Resistance to evil is of course one of the first duties. Our Lord Himself lived one long campaign against evil. Without compunction He drove evil spirits out of their unlawful possessions. He violently drove out of the Temple those who were profaning it. Submission to personal wrong is one thing: allowance of evil-doing quite another.

Our Lord expects us to bring a grain of common sense and the liberty of the spirit to the interpretation of

His commands. A popular speaker must be one-sided. To introduce modifying conditions and minute qualifications of a broad law is to leave no impression at all on the mind of his audience. He who paints a picture which is meant to strike the masses must paint with a large brush and in strong colours. It must be judged by the effect. Does it leave behind it the impression intended? What is the result of our Lord's picture of the ideal human life? It leaves the impression that He believes in the conquering power of love; that retaliation is condemned; that any anxiety about our worldly condition which obliterates faith in the Father is unworthy. In point of fact, these precepts have brought home to the mind of Christendom the necessity of cultivating the spirit they express, and they have done so with tenfold the force which would have been exerted by prosaic instructions. They depict an ideal. And, as Dr. D. M. Ross says: 'It is one of the secrets of the attractiveness of Christ as an ethical teacher, that He holds up before us ideals so great that we can never fully compass them but are humbled in their presence, but yet so congruous with what is best in us that in struggling up towards them we know we are realising our truest manhood.'

These precepts, then, have accomplished their purpose in giving a concrete, easily remembered expression of an ideal which Christian men will always seek to realise. They are of the nature of proverbs, which the dull logical mind, concerning itself only with the literal shell, will break its teeth upon; but which honesty sucks the truth out of and converts into invigorating blood. They are of use only to those who desire to make the most of them; and he who recognises that there is teaching here which must not be lightly passed by as impracticable, because it is difficult of application, will not find it impossible to discriminate between those cases in which a literal fulfilment is obligatory and those in which the Spirit of the Master is better satisfied without a literal obedience.

The true solvent of the problems raised by the Lord's words, the true key to their interpretation, is the great principle underlying them. They are various exemplifications or illustrations of the fundamental law of love. By this they must be interpreted. And love gives us a frontier in both directions. Forgiveness till seventy-times seven does not exhaust the inexhaustible compassion of love. 'Love suffereth long.' Love gives and gives and gives. Like God Himself, love gives 'simply'; gives without thought of reward or even of recognition. We must learn to hold our possessions, our faculties, our time, ourselves for the common good. Only by entering into Christ's spirit of love can we obey His precepts. On the other hand, love warns us against thoughtless, indiscriminate giving. Love is compelled to refuse as often as to give. To supply men with the means of destroying themselves body and soul by gambling or drinking is not the dictate of true love. To pauperise men by relieving them of parental responsibilities, to encourage them to shirk work and turn loafers and loungers is certainly no part of Christian duty. This one principle covers and governs all our relations to this present world. For it is only he who considers himself a member of the vast body of society, and who really has some true consideration for his fellow men, who can truly hold himself and all his possessions at the disposal of the common good. To what extent he may hold this world's 'treasure' is a question for each man's conscience.

II
BY THE REV. PROFESSOR JAMES DENNEY, D.D.

EVERY one has felt the difficulty of interpreting the Sermon on the Mount, and many have felt also that the kind of difficulty which at once puts out the auditor and fascinates him must in some sense be calculated by the Speaker. At all events, it falls in admirably with His purpose. The aim of Jesus is to compel in His hearers an interest as vivid as His own in the great concerns of which He speaks. He wishes to provoke a powerful reaction in their moral intelligence, and nothing is more fitted to do this than that series of striking utterances which has given commentators so much to do, and has caused such searchings of heart in multitudes who care nothing for commentators, but long to be loyal to Christ. What ought to be our attitude toward the startling, challenging words of Jesus in the Sermon?

Two things may be said by way of preliminary. No solution of difficulties is sound which questions the universal scope of Jesus' words. It is true that the disciples are distinguished at the beginning from the multitudes at the end, but the morality of the Sermon is not meant for one class in such a sense as to exclude others from its claims. If the multitude were not disciples, they might have been and ought to have been, and when Jesus speaks it is for every one who has ears to hear. No doubt there are special vocations in the world, and in the Kingdom of God, that have special obligations attached to them, but these are not in view in the Sermon. It is spoken in the common air which all men breathe, and if it is binding on any, it is binding to precisely the same intent on all. Further, no solution is admissible which on any pretext reduces the words of Jesus to moral commonplace. Whatever they signify, they are something else than this. The keynote of the Sermon is *Except your righteousness exceed,* or *What do ye more than others?* 'More than others' is in Greek *peritton.* The words of Socrates, Aristotle said, had always something *peritton* about them—something over and above what even the same words would have carried in the lips of other men. This is signally true of the words of Jesus in the Sermon. If we reduce them to a meaning in which we lose the sense of the extraordinary, we have missed the mark. Intellectually, they challenge us. Emotionally, they vibrate with passion. Ethically, they suggest if they do not define a new standard the height and range of which make themselves felt through endless imperfections of intelligence.

The only positive rule of interpretation is that words must be interpreted out of the mind of the speaker. It is something even to remember that it is a speaker with whom we are dealing, not a writer. A writer is removed by some degrees from the situation which makes rhetoric, with all its resources of paradox, hyperbole and passion, inevitable. He may fairly be treated more literally than a speaker. But a speaker with his hearers before him knows that something else than literalism is demanded. He realises that to a large extent his business is not to elucidate ideas, but to communicate emotion. He has to transfer to others his own sense of the transcendent importance of certain interests, and to kindle in them the conviction that to secure such interests no effort and no sacrifice are too great. This is the situation in which we must conceive Jesus to speak. He stands among us with a sense of God, of God's fatherly love for men, of God's interest in human life and claims upon it—with a sense of the ultimate realities of our situation, and therefore of what ought to be the ultimate motives in it—such as has no parallel in our knowledge; and it is from the consciousness of all this that He speaks in the Sermon on the Mount. His words are only intelligible as partial revelations of Himself: it is through Him we must understand them, as much as through them we understand Him. To read them as if they were the statutory injunctions of an Act of Parliament, that had been brought to the required precision by carefully considered amendments, is infallibly to go astray. They are not statutory injunctions at all: they are jets of living flame. They are not meant to save us the trouble of thinking, but to kindle in us the most intense and vivid thought.

This rule of interpretation may be illustrated by reference to two of the most persistent difficulties in the Sermon on the Mount. The first is the law of non-retaliation. 'I say unto you, that ye resist not evil: but whosoever shall smite thee on thy right cheek, turn to him the other also. And if any man will sue thee at the law and take away thy coat, let him have thy cloke also. And whosoever shall compel thee to go a mile, go with him twain. Give to him that asketh thee, and from him that would borrow of thee turn not thou away.' Nothing is more obvious than the feeling with which these words are charged. The subject is one in which the speaker is deeply concerned: no language is too strong—may we not say no hyperbole too extravagant?—to convey His meaning. But what is His meaning? What is the situation in view of which He utters Himself so paradoxically, with such various illustration, with such reiterated emphasis? Is there not reason to think it a situation fundamentally distinct from that in which it is sometimes suggested that literal or statutory obedience should be rendered to His words? The modern Christian who reads the Sermon on the Mount has no experience of the kind of injuries here described. No one has ever struck him on the face, or swindled him at law, or impressed his services by force. But the world in which Jesus contemplated His disciples living was different. It was a world in which persecution was inevitable, a world in which we must through much tribulation enter into the Kingdom of God. The typical Christian of the New Testament is the martyr, the man who takes up his cross daily—who goes out every morning, as we might say, with a rope round his neck, ready to die unresisting the most ignominious death, if it comes to him as he follows Jesus. It is one application of this, the fundamental truth of Christian morality, that we find in the various sayings about nonresistance. The situation which it contemplates the disciple has simply to accept. The typical Christian is the martyr, and there is no such thing as being a martyr by halves. No matter what the wrong may be which at any particular moment the disciple has to endure—whether it be in the region of property or in that of honour, whether it be more or less insolent in form—there is only one spirit in which it ought to be accepted, the martyr spirit. On the assumption that the wrong is inevitable—which is, throughout, the New Testament assumption—anything else is at one ineffective and undignified. To deny this is not only to make these particular words of Jesus of no effect, it is to set aside the inspiration of His Life and Example as a whole.

But what about the application of the words to all the forms of wrong which are perpetrated in a society like ours? Are we bound, because we are Christians, to let evil-doers have their way without restraint? Are we really to give to every one who holds out his hand? In answering such questions we have no guide but conscience, and conscience refuses even to look at the affirmative answer. It is on moral grounds that we say these words are not to be read as statutes. No man could fulfil a moral calling in the world at all—still less could the moral calling of societies be fulfilled—if the person and the property of human beings were to be at the mercy of the unscrupulous, the violent, and the ineffective. It is not honouring Jesus to read His words so. Just as little would it be honouring Jesus to set His words aside as if they could have no meaning for us at all. The words are still original, exacting and clear. They are a defiant way of asserting that even when he is wronged the Christian is under the law of love. He is never under any other law. Let the wrong be as brutal, as ingenious, as wanton, insulting, tyrannical as human badness can make it, the Christian is never to relapse from love in dealing with his enemy to some lower principle which he may call justice, still less to the natural selfish passion of revenge. He is to find in love alone his impulse and his guide, and he is to go all lengths with love. That is the impression which the vehemence of Jesus leaves and is designed to leave upon our minds, but it is a pure unintelligence to read His paradoxical words as if they were a statute for love. Love must be a law to itself. Jesus did not say these things to save us the trouble of thinking what love requires, but to compel us to take the trouble; to compel us, in a word, to take on ourselves the responsibility of deciding, on the Christian level, and under the Christian motive, what our duty is. We are not under law, even the law of His words: we are under grace, which means the inspiration of His whole being; and we fail in our duty to those who most wantonly injure us if even in our dealings with them we let other motives than those which this inspiration supplies determine our conduct.

Analogous considerations apply to the interpretation of the second saying in the Sermon which seems at present to trouble many and perhaps to please more— 'Lay not up for yourselves treasures upon the earth.' This is far from being the only word of Jesus about money; it is no exaggeration to say that there is more about money in the Gospels than about any other single subject. It is in the same key too, as a great deal more. Jesus was profoundly impressed by the power of money to engross and absorb the heart. He saw it become the god of its owners. Men worshipped it, and did anything for it. No language was too strong to declare its perils. 'It is easier for a camel to go through a needle's eye than for a rich man to enter into the Kingdom of God.' We must remember this when we read the Sermon on the Mount, and if we do, perhaps we shall not be so quick to assume that St. Paul's formula—'they that have as though they possessed not'—exactly covers the thought of Jesus. Possibly the Apostle had not the Master's intense feeling of the dangers connected with riches, and thought it easier than it really is for the average man to have as though he possessed not. But keeping this in mind, it is surely a transparent mistake to argue that Jesus in His character as Legislator here sets up a statute against riches from which it is an immediate inference that those who are rich are living in contempt of His law. We need only to look at the whole sentence—'Lay not up for yourselves treasures on the earth, but lay up for yourselves treasures in heaven'—to see how false this literalism is. We have precisely the same kind of sentence in the fourth Gospel:

'Labour not for the meat which perisheth, but for that which endureth unto life everlasting.' Will anybody be found to argue from the first half of this that Jesus forbids us to work for our living? And if not, surely it is evident in both cases what we have to do with is a matter of comparison and precedence. Man's chief end, Jesus tells us, is *not* to be rich here, but to be rich toward God; his true life does *not* consist in the abundance of the things which he possesses, but in something entirely independent of possessions. These are things to be laid to heart by the rich, undoubtedly; if they have learned anything from Jesus, they will have learned to dread the temptations incident to wealth, and to resist them by generosity, humility toward God, and reverence for the human worth of all men. But it is inept to say that a man cannot be a Christian and rich. If riches have their terrible temptations, so has poverty. Worldly care is as great an enemy to the Kingdom as the intoxication of wealth, and *Take no thought for your life* is a saying that tests the poor as severely as *Lay not up treasures for yourselves on the earth* does the rich. What rich and poor, according to Jesus, are alike tempted to forget is the Fatherly providence of God, and man's dependence on it. We must think, we must look to the future, we must insure ourselves and those dependent on us as we can. But we should do it as those who are insuring *with* providence, not—as many men, both rich and poor, do—as though we were insuring *against* providence. How many people think they would become religious and have time for God and His Kingdom and righteousness, *if only* their future were a little secure, their standing in the world independent! As though God and His Kingdom and righteousness were not the primary concerns, and the recognition of our absolute dependence on Him the beginning of religion.

The key to the Sermon on the Mount is the thought of God as Father, and the common relation of ourselves and all our fellow-men to Him as children. Jesus knows what this involves, but His boldest words do not tell it. They summon us, rather, to realise it for ourselves; they are like sudden far-reaching flashes of light that show the direction in which the conscience has to travel. But they are not statutes. They have to deal with morality, and morality is not the region of statute, but of inspiration, freedom, and responsibility. The mind of Jesus in the Sermon will be reached, not when we keep His words as we observe the terms of an Act of Parliament, but when the consciousness of God in our hearts is like what it was in His, and when we find in that consciousness the inspiration of all our judgments and actions. This is the freedom of the spirit which St. Paul understood so well, a freedom without which there is no Christianity, but which is not bound by any statute, even by a statutory interpretation of the words of Christ.

III
BY THE REV. JAMES MOFFATT, D.D.

THE FLAG OR THE RUDDER

IN the ninth chapter of *The Professor at the Breakfast-Table*, Dr. Oliver Wendell Holmes makes one of his characters ask indignantly, 'Can any man look round and see what Christian countries are now doing, and how they are governed, and what is the general condition of society, without seeing that Christianity is the flag under which the world sails, and not the rudder that steers its course?' Whether one sees this or not, the look round is healthy. It indicates a sensitiveness of conscience, a searching of heart, a courage of mind, which are all to the good. Every now and then an uprising of concern seems to stir within the Christian society, as to whether it may not be acquiescing tacitly in ideas and practices which are irreconcilable with its avowed character. Have we any right to call ourselves still Christians, men ask, in anger or in pathos, according to their mood? Is not modern civilisation, in manners and commerce alike, organised on lines which render a genuine obedience to the Christian standard impracticable? Are not the driving and guiding powers of life as we see it lived, non-Christian, or Christian in name alone? Were this the case, it would undoubtedly be better to lower the flag, rather than sail dishonestly under false colours. Better the pang of parting with a time-honoured but antiquated pennant, than self-deception and self-satisfaction. In the long run it might even happen that a sincere, straight course of life, owning no formal adherence to Christianity, would be found to approximate in many essentials to the Christian ethical standard. The heroic alternative to pulling down the flag would be a change of rudder, or— to drop the metaphor—an alteration of the whole social order, with a view to realising more perfectly the Christian ideal of the Sermon on the Mount, with which that order seems to conflict so glaringly.

The spirit of the latter course, which actuates the literal interpretation of the Sermon, is to be respected. It is robust and logical, at least. Morally it is many degrees nobler than an attitude of languid or hectic admiration for Christ's precepts, which is accompanied by no sort of practical attempt to realise them, an attitude in which people can insulate their consciences by paying sterile homage to the lofty principles of Jesus as too ideal for common use. But the spirit of a movement or method may be commendable, while its basis is unsound, and, though no sane person would deny the discrepancies between modern life and Christianity, it is a fair question whether the interpretation which involves this root-and-branch treatment of a supposed discord, may not be actuated by some exaggerated conceptions or biassed by certain preconceived ideas. Mischief and misery are often the result of disobedience to an acknowledged standard. But more often than is realised, they ooze into life from the acceptance of some wrong ideal. A false or narrow view of duty, arrived at in all honesty, may be responsible for widespread trouble in the church and in society, and one function of historical criticism is to enable the plain, spontaneous instincts of Christianity to correct themselves in the light of experience and intelligence, by taking into consideration such features and factors of interpretation as the relativity of language and the power as well as the duty of reinterpreting ideals, even in the act of admitting their binding force upon the conscience.

To many, within as well as without the Christian church, arguments of this nature will probably appear irrelevant. They may even be dubbed 'shuffling.' What is this, we are told, but a process of casuistry or of ethical evasion? Does it not represent an endeavour to adjust the severe demands of the gospel to the laxer, conventional tastes of an age which is content to have Christianity as an embroidered flag, but resolved to possess a rudder of its own shaping? Undoubtedly such motives have now and then operated in theorising upon the Sermon. They may do so, almost unknown to men; or they may be leading the mind, though one is slow to admit it even to oneself, to draw up reasons for some course of action which has been determined already upon extra-Christian reasons. Such, however, are the abuses, not the condemnation, of the method. These risks have to be taken. They do not serve to invalidate the principle that the history of the moral consciousness in Christendom and the data of the enlightened conscience form part of that context apart from which no proper focus for estimating the permanent message of the Sermon can be acquired. Historical criticism by itself has comparatively little help to offer in this matter. It may point out the difference of *métier* between the two versions of the Sermon; it may clear up difficulties of detail; it may show how both presuppose some common source, whose general spirit is more accurately preserved by Matthew. But, after all is said and done, the ethical demands are unaltered, and the main contribution of historical criticism to the interpretation of the Sermon consists in the reminder that no reading of it can hope to be accurate or inspiring, which divorces its message from the original situation or from the lasting relationship of Jesus and His disciples.

Now the literalist interpretation of the Sermon on the Mount involves isolation from the ordinary standards which govern the interpretation of all pregnant, popular statements, modern as well as ancient. One of these standards is the distinction between a statute or principle and a rule of conduct. No one has put this more cogently than Newman, in his lecture *On Preaching the Gospel.* 'Principles,' he observes, 'are great truths or laws which embody in them the character of a system, enable us to estimate it, and indirectly guide us in practice.' The word 'indirectly' is used on purpose. For, as the writer proceeds to indicate, 'it is a characteristic of such statements of principles to be short, pointed, strong, and often somewhat paradoxical in appearance. Such, for example, is the political maxim, which has a clear and true meaning, but in form is startling, "The King can do no wrong"; or in physics, that "nature abhors a vacuum." They are laws or exhibitions of general truths: and not directly practical. I mean, a man will be sure to get into difficulty or error if he attempts to use them as guides in matters of conduct and duty. They mean nothing, or something wide of the truth, taken as literal directions. They are like the sun in the heavens, too high, too distant, to light your lamp by, though indirectly and secondarily useful even for that.' This is almost too obvious a truth to require emphasis. It has been alluded to already in the previous articles of the present series, and its application to the Sermon on the Mount simply involves common sense, just as its cognate feature—an allowance for what may be termed the Oriental hyperbole, or the pictorial and parabolic shape of it— demands no more than an elementary acquaintance with historical criticism. To translate the Sermon literally into the life of Western civilisation would be in some respects as much a misinterpretation as a literal English version of its Greek, or of any ancient classic, would be. The letter would be preserved at the expense of the spirit. A word-for-word translation of some Greek or Latin passage is generally further from the real meaning than one which allows, by the use of a wise freedom, for the differences of idiom between the two languages. Well, the same principle holds of translation into act. To get a precise equivalent in conduct for some of the hard sayings of the Sermon is a much more elaborate and exacting task than many literalists seem to realise; its adequate execution demands that the practical Western interpreter, in his very desire to preserve the spirit and essence of an original which is neither wholly figurative nor esoteric, shall know where and how far to sit loose to modes of thought and expression involved in the original Oriental setting. This may not carry us very far. But at least it suggests that to distort the Sermon into a programme of eccentric idealism is only a shade better than to flatten it into a moral commonplace, and that the alternatives before the Christian conscience, when confronted by the Sermon on the one side and modern commerce, legislation, and warfare on the other, need not be wholesale acceptance or wholesale repudiation. Complacency and iconoclasm, the later and earlier attitudes of the ordinary mind towards such problems, may be the logical policies open to those who accept the Sermon as a series of statutory enactments. Take it as a Utopia and worship society; take it literally and sacrifice society: these constitute the normal dilemma hurled at the conscientious, perplexed modern. It is at least something to feel that the dilemma rests on a false reading of the Sermon, and that the issue need not be quite so simple and desperate. Hard sayings may be hard to understand and easy to obey, or easy to understand and hard to obey. The Sermon contains examples of both. These examples are probably destined to operate with far-reaching effect upon the church and society of to-day. But, without blunting their heroic edge, historical criticism claims to show that they are not quite so alien to the circumstances and ideals of the enlightened conscience as at first appears.

Again, as a number of writers have correctly seen, the literal interpretation of the Sermon suffers from a failure to read such words of Jesus in the light of His life and of the rest of His teaching, to say nothing of the primitive Christian churches. Here historical criticism steps in also to point out that such a wider survey limits and qualifies the statements of the Sermon at more than one point, however it may ratify them on the whole. This survey would involve a discussion alike of the relation between the historical and the authoritative elements in the gospel, and of the general ethics of Jesus, both of which lie beyond the purview of the present paper. But in any case, whatever view be taken of the relation, *e.g.* between Paul's ethic and that of Jesus—so far as the latter can be traced in the synoptic gospels—the Sermon on the Mount, for all its compact and impressive character, cannot be taken as the sufficient expression of Christian practice, any more than the parable of the Prodigal Son. It is not, it was never meant to be, a moral *vade-mecum*. Tolstoy's great effort to make it the pith of the New Testament was foredoomed to failure, splendid as the failure was. It was a *tour-de-force*. Christianity, as Matthew Arnold urged in his criticism of the Russian writer—a criticism which curiously anticipates one of the points recently made by Loisy against Harnack—'Christianity cannot be packed into any set of commandments. It is a mistake, and may lead to much error, to exhibit any series of maxims, even those of the Sermon on the Mount, as the ultimate sum and formula into which Christianity may be run up.... The most important and fruitful utterances of Jesus are not things which can be drawn up as a table of stiff and stark external commands, but the things which have most soul in them.'

This broadens out into a further and final aspect of the Sermon as an utterance of Jesus Christ to His disciples. The more inward its application, the more exacting it is. The more it is taken as the pressure of Christ's soul upon the soul and conscience of His church, the more pregnant will be its effects. Now, on this view, the literal interpretation of the Sermon is not severe enough. To most people it may seem a paradox to say so, a contradiction in terms. What could be harder, they retort, than to obey to the letter such commands as *Resist not evil, Give to every man that asketh of thee, Lay not up for yourselves treasures upon earth?* Your method of so-called spiritual interpretation, on the other hand, leaves the individual free to pick and choose as he pleases, and, by an arbitrary, eclectic scheme of ethics, to arrange a life which may be comfortable and even refined, improving and perhaps innocent enough, but which is at most demi-semi-Christian. The rejoinder to such a charge is both ample and easy, but the core of it lies in the principle that, whatever may lurk within the mind of particular individuals, the truly spiritual—or historical if you will—reading of the Sermon cannot afford to isolate it from that relationship of Christ to Christians apart from which it must infallibly, though sometimes gloriously, be misconceived. This is not to set up a temporary and fluctuating shelter of compromise. Admittedly, its results vary not only from age to age, with the varying degrees of faithfulness to Christ, but within each age; for, without holding that any of the precepts in the Sermon are counsels of perfection, we are entitled to say that special circumstances may dictate a special vocation for this or that individual. Yet the common principle remains, the principle of facing the demands of One who meets us where we are, quickened as well as handicapped by past generations, the principle, *i.e.* of responsibility, not simply for obeying the light we receive, but for the light we do not receive. The two parts of this responsibility are intimately related. Who can estimate the light that would be thrown on such problems as those of commercial ethics or international morality, were the church, and the individuals who compose the church, to act more resolutely upon those maxims of the Sermon which are in moral, not in intellectual, discord with current thought and practice? I do not maintain that all the further problems would yield at a touch to this method. But surely this undeviating recognition of a tie between Christians and Him who speaks to them not only about, but through, the personal experience of their own day, is the sole atmosphere in which fuller light can reasonably be expected upon questions as yet perplexing to the mind and conscience of Christendom.

When Jesus, an honoured guest in the house of Simon the Pharisee, noted his host's tacit disapproval of His own attitude towards the penitent woman, He said to him, *Simon, I have somewhat to say unto thee.* Simon replied, *Master, say on.* What the Master had to say proved unpalatable and surprising enough; we are not told whether Simon had the grace and courage to act upon it, or whether his permission to speak was no more than formal courtesy. But the point is that Christ similarly enters the modern home and church and social order, not necessarily to find them incapable of adjustment to His spirit, but often to find that, with all their outward deference to Him, standards and traditions of conduct are in operation which bear cruelly upon some members, and therefore are at variance with His own temper and mind. Of such practices we may be frequently oblivious. Custom has deadened any qualms of conscience we ever felt in the matter. Such usages are interwoven with the social order into which we are born. They are part and parcel of our civilisation, and many grow up to share the prevalent notions of morality and Christian principle, without seriously questioning their compatibility with the Christian standard which they profess, in good faith it may be, to welcome and respect. The world, even the religious world, has its mould and sometimes it is with a positive shock of surprise that we find this mould quietly and firmly broken by what is the rising spirit of Christ within the individual or the social conscience. It is much if we can say, *Master, say on.* It is more, it is everything, if we attempt, at all costs to pride and prejudice, to rearrange life under that moral authority of Christ in virtue of which He moves to revise or recast our conventional standards of thought and action. And that sensitiveness of conscience, that recognition of the Speaker's authority rather than of any legal and verbal obligation, is what the method of spiritual interpretation, in its genuine form, cherishes. Its object is the growth of those instincts in religious character from which the finest obedience springs. A mere precept, or set of precepts, we can take away with us. We can put them into force, literally, if we choose. But they soon exhaust themselves. They are inelastic, they become stereotyped. We come to the end of them, feeling perhaps that the world has outgrown their usefulness. And not only, in many cases, do they result in a curiously barren, or at least inadequate, line of moral conduct, but they leave the soul blank. A man, *e.g.* may be a communist without being a Christian, or at least a better Christian for it. The end is formalism, the bondage of the exterior—a bondage which is really the mildest in the world, because it soon becomes a yoke of words or of precepts done simply on the ground that they are sanctioned by use and wont. The spiritual interpretation of Christ's words takes a harder and a higher way. In its very ardour to see the selfishness and worldliness of modern life reduced, it steadily refuses to isolate these words from the entire, living spirit of Christ witnessing to the spirit of man through the history and experience of the race. It never can see an end of all perfection, for it 'turns the Sermon on the Mount,' as Dean Church observed, 'from a code of precepts into the expressions and instances of a character. Its words do not stand by themselves; they are not as the definite commandments of a law; they cannot be represented or exhausted by any rules; they have their interpretation and their reason in that divine temper which had come with Jesus Christ to restore the world.' Now, what can be more exacting? A saying is never so hard in the letter as it is in the spirit, and this is to take Christ's words in the spirit. What, again, can be more hopeful and fruitful than such an attitude towards the Sermon and its Speaker? Hopeful and fruitful just on the score of its unabated pressure. It is hard upon the mind, for it refuses to cut the Gordian knot of ethical perplexity by the sword either of mental indifference or of emotion. It does not seek to save us the trouble of thinking. It recognises that for the individual, and much more for the social conscience, far more than a stimulant of emotion is needed. Patient study of the problem historically, inquiry into our ethical environment, with its ideals, achievements, and errors, and a willingness to weigh and to reconsider many factors of the question—all these are elements in that divine service of the mind which is substituted by the spiritual interpretation of the Sermon for any unreflecting attempts to rush the solution of such problems as are presented by the juxtaposition of Christ's words and modern life. And this labour of the mind, harder for the solution of social or international questions than for the individual life, is bound up with an equally severe demand upon the will and conscience. All such inquiries presuppose honesty and sincerity. None can enter on them with any prospect of success, unless he is prepared to act upon their results, be these what they may. *Master, say on*—is the falsest of all acts of homage from the lips of those who are secretly resolved to do no more than they are doing or can do without serious disturbance of the *status quo*. The spiritual interpretation of the Master's words, starting from the conception of man's sonship to the Father, is only justified as it is ready to let the new light rearrange the old life, no matter what inconvenience and shame may ensue. But, when it is prepared for this, it feels, and has the right to say, that any purely literal interpretation fails to present a sufficiently large and living Christ to men; for even though the latter method is often an honest attempt to secure that perpetual revision of life which is implicit in the conception of Christ's authority, the attempt is misguided. Its stimulus does not rise from deep enough sources. Its end is a communion with the obsolete rather than with the unseen elements of Christianity. Whereas the spiritual method is pregnant, hopeful, and alert, for this if for no other reason that it endeavours above all to be faithful at once to the historical environment of Christ's words and to the living spirit of Him who rises above the first as well as above the twentieth century, with the remoulding message: *I have somewhat to say unto thee.*

Similar Titles from CrossReach

The Sermon on the Mount

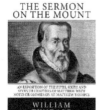

William Tyndale

"Here hast thou, dear reader, an exposition upon the fifth, sixth, and seventh chapters of Matthew, wherein Christ, our spiritual Isaac, diggeth again the wells of Abraham: which wells the scribes and Pharisees, those wicked and spiteful Philistines, had stopped and filled up with the earth of their false expositions. He openeth the kingdom of heaven, which they had shut up that other men should not enter, as they themselves had no lust to go in. He restoreth the key of knowledge, which they had taken away, and broken the wards, with wresting the text, contrary to his due and natural course, with their false glosses. He plucketh away from the face of Moses the veil which the scribes and Pharisees had spread thereon, that no man might perceive the brightness of his countenance. He weedeth out the thorns and bushes of their pharisaical glosses, wherewith they had stopped up the narrow way and strait gate, that few could find them.

Read here the words of Christ with this exposition following, and thou shalt see the law, faith, and works, restored each to his right use and true meaning; and thereto, the clear difference between the spiritual regiment and the temporal; and shalt have an entrance and open way into the rest of all the scripture. Wherein, and in all other things, the Spirit of verity guide thee and thine understanding. So be it."

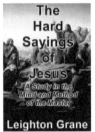

Hard Sayings of Jesus Christ: A Study in the Mind and Method of the Master

Leighton Grane

Few will fail to find the very heart and soul of the biblical body in the words of "The Word of God" Himself. By this, the core of Christianity, its claim on the hearts and lives of men must finally be judged. But in order to judge it is necessary to understand. Therefore before all things it seems necessary to set the Words of Jesus in their own proper historical light in order to arrive at the meaning they conveyed to those who first heard them, for this alone can safely be accounted the primary meaning of their Speaker.

Among the authoritative and reason-compelling Words of Jesus Christ, however, some undoubtedly cause trouble to thinking minds. Appearing on a shallow acquaintance either impracticable or reasonless, they not only fail of authority but sow the seeds of doubt. The object, therefore, of this book is the lessening of such perplexities by setting forth the principles which seem to elucidate the Teaching of the Master. It is an attempt to construe the meaning of some of the more striking of Christ's "hard sayings." Others, here untouched, might no doubt easily be cited. But the aim of the writer has not been to exhaust the verbal difficulties in the recorded utterances of our Lord. He has rather sought to examine the Master's method, and to illustrate its underlying principles by a number of examples perhaps sufficient to enable the reader to apply those principles in solving other problems for himself.

Who Moved the Stone?
Frank Morison

...The third day he rose again from the dead...

What?! Really?!

Frank Morison, a former sceptic, originally had intended in driving the final nail in Jesus' coffin, only to realise he actually had risen from the dead! Here is an honest account of a man who finally submits to the weight of evidence that Jesus truly did rise from the dead. You may not agree with everything he says or with all of his conclusions but you will be deeply challenged and thrilled to see just how strong the case for New Testament Christianity truly is.

"Fascinating in its lucid, its almost incontrovertibly, appeal to the reason." — J. D. Beresford

"It is as though a skilled advocate, entirely convinced of the truth of his case, were unravelling the threads of some mystery ... It has the supreme merit o frankness and sincerity" — The Sunday Times

"I owe Morison a great debt of gratitude. Who Moved the Stone? was an important early link in a long chain of evidence that God used to bring me into his kingdom.

Morison's stirring intellectual exploration of the historical record proved to be an excellent starting point for my spiritual investigation." —From the foreword of another edition by Lee Strobel

Made in United States
Troutdale, OR
09/10/2023

12798053R00033